Introduction

Little Barn Owls Nursery & Farm School is based in Horsham on a workir
large garden with an allotment and farm school with rabbits, guinea pigs
pig that roams around the garden with children every day. We have two p.   . .....os called
'Ateliers' that home high end creative materials and resources. Working in   ..c spaces are Atelieristi,
Professional Artists that work with the children daily.

At Little Barn Owls, we live by a set of core values and principles that reflect the image of the child as a strong, capable and competent being that is driven by curiosity and the desire to connect with the world around them from birth. Children are active researchers that are capable of constructing their own learning, driven by their own questions. Engaging and connecting deeply with the environment and others around them enable children to make sense of their place in the world.

Our pedagogical approach is principally inspired by the Infant-toddler centres and Pre-schools of the Municipality of Reggio Emilia in Northern Italy. We adopt an enquiry-based learning approach which is committed to listening to children and helping them develop their fascinations and theories into long term projects. These theories, questions and discoveries are listened to by educators and reflected upon by adults and children who make important decisions about time, spaces and resources to enable the continuation of children's research. Our approach pays close attention to the environment viewing it as 'the third teacher.' The environment is recognised as a tool to inspire, engage and connect with, providing opportunities to delve into fascinations and develop ideas using a wide range of materials and creative mediums.

This 10 month project took place within the pre-school room and on occasion within the Digital Atelier. The provocations set within the Digital Atelier were also set in the main nursery room, demonstrating that the Atelier space is not essential to engage children in ideas that they are closely connected to. Our pre-school spaces are very dynamic and reflective of children's thoughts and ideas. The different spaces allow for both independent and collaborative engagement over time. Spaces for children to come back to their drawings and creations to add to, modify and critique their ideas and share them day after day.

The documentation included within this book aims to make visible the learning processes, theories and representations of the children's fascination with themselves, their anatomy, their mind and their identity.

Protagonists - Children involved
(Followed by age in years and months)

Sebastian Alldridge	3.4	Madeline Hedger	3.10
Eloise Appleby	3.1	Max Henderson	3.11
Reef Baker	2.10	Lara Hinchey	3.8
Tristan Baty	3.11	Theodore (Teddy) Hoffman	4.0
Isabella (Izzy) Bassett	2.7	Frederik (Freddie) Howells	4.8
Jude Baxter	4.2	Jack Howells	3.1
George Bean	4.7	Madeleine Hughes	3.1
Joe Bending	2.11	Thomas Hughes	3.1
Thea Bishop	3.4	Dylan Hurdle	4.4
Eden Botevyle	2.6	Bethany Jackson	4.5
Olivia Brotherwood	2.7	Jack Jones	4.9
Henry Brothwood	3.2	Eva King	4.5
Ruby Catling	3.10	Sebastian King	4.5
Luke Chambers	3.3	Cameron Klingenberg	3.2
Arthur Chapman	3.9	Reuben Macauley	3.2
Dominic Clarke	4.4	Benjamin Martin	3.10
Thomas Collingwood	4.2	Lucas Midtboe van Schalkwyk	3.11
Niamh Davenport	3.4	Archie Milton	3.8
Beau Douglas	3.10	Charlie Minall	3.11
Daniel Drinkall	3.5	Samuel Morris	2.8
Eva Eade	4.7	Harry Mustard	4.4
Benjamin Ellis	2.10	Alex Neligan	3.7
Jack Etheridge-Smith	4.7	Emily Owens	4.6
Amy Everitt	3.11	Ria Panchal	3.8
Molly Fairs	3.1	Elizabeth Patience	3.4
Summer Faulding	3.3	Lottie Pearce	2.6
Emily Farmelo	4.8	Oscar Phillips	3.5
Gwen Faulkes	2.8	Hayden Pretorius	3.1
Joshua Godding	2.10	Lucas Prodger	3.9
Rowan Gooding	4.7	Maksim Scoville	3.5
Zach Goodliffe	4.5	Hugo Sears	3.7
Cleo Gorringe	2.11	Rowan Sillett	2.11
Cameron Griffiths	4.6	Isabelle Simpson	2.4
Isla Hardy	3.0	Soloman Smallwood-Brown	3.11
Maia Harrison	2.11	Darcey Smith	3.0
Arlo Hart	4.8	Poppy Smith	2.10

Lead Educators - Charlotte Middleton and Jodie Webber
Written by Charlotte Middleton and Jodie Webber
Edited by Hayley Peacock
Book Design by Dillon Howling, Charlotte Middleton, Jodie Webber and Hayley Peacock

Brain

Whilst a group of children were composing with scrap material on our outdoor atelier — a large platform and an array of open ended resources to construct with — Bethany (4.5 yrs) announces...

"Do you know, we have worlds in our heads and tunnels in our minds?"

A provoking thought that lead to interesting discussion and debate at our daily reflection meeting with the children. After a moment to ponder this divergent idea, Brady (4 yrs) adds,

"No, we have brains in our heads"

Reflecting on these thoughts, educators decided to enable the children to build upon their thoughts and represent brains through different languages of expression, including paint, wire and wool for composing.

"The brain is in my body, in my head"
Joshua (2.10 yrs)

"These slots are veins in the brain"
Louis (4.10 yrs) whilst painting.

"This is my brain, it's got bendy lines, that's why I think" Beau (3.10 yrs)

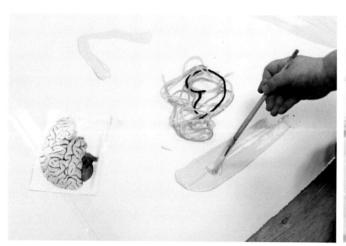 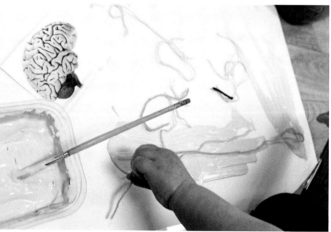

"Lines in your brain tell you to move, where to go. In your brain there's lines, like your moves" Ellis (4.5 yrs)

Drawing of lines in the brain by Ellis

Digital Microscope

We offered the children use of a digital microscope as a 'lens to see inside' themselves.

The digital microscope became a way for the children to 'see what's inside' their bodies. The children place the digital microscopes on different parts of their bodies and stared in awe at the projections on the wall.

"I can see my brain, look!" Dylan (4.4 yrs)

To support this enquiry, a parent donated an anatomical model. This sparked questions and ideas about 'what's inside us' and what organs we have?

"I have one hundred hearts" Seb (3.4 yrs)

"What do one hundred

hearts do?" Educator

"They make you go all movey!" Seb

Identity

During morning discussion into how we are different and what unites us, Emily O (4.6 yrs) announces..

"Our hands are all the same"

Charlotte (educator) asked the other children whether they thought their hands were the same, to which the children were unsure. Charlotte suggested they research their hands in more depth to gain more understanding, then they can decide.

Emily O (4.6 yrs), Emily F (4.8 yrs) and Amy (3.11 yrs) were given a camera to take photographs of their hands for them to inspect. These images were projected onto the wall. The children took note of the slight differences in skin tone.

The same group of children ventured into the digital atelier where they used ink pads to print their fingerprints onto acetate on the lightbox, taking a close look at the difference in print patterns.

The group then used a digital microscope to look at their hands and fingerprints in microscopic detail.

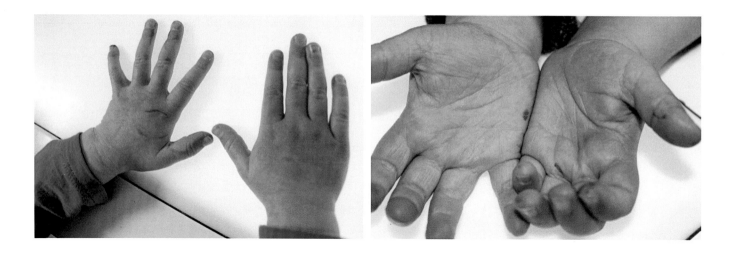

Emily F (4.8 yrs) decided to use a digital scanner to scan the palm of her hands to create an image on the computer. With support the group enlarged the photograph and discussed the differences and similarities within their scanned images.

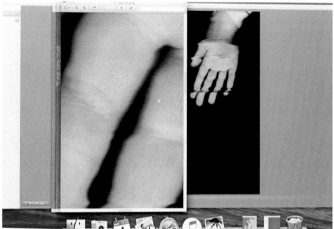

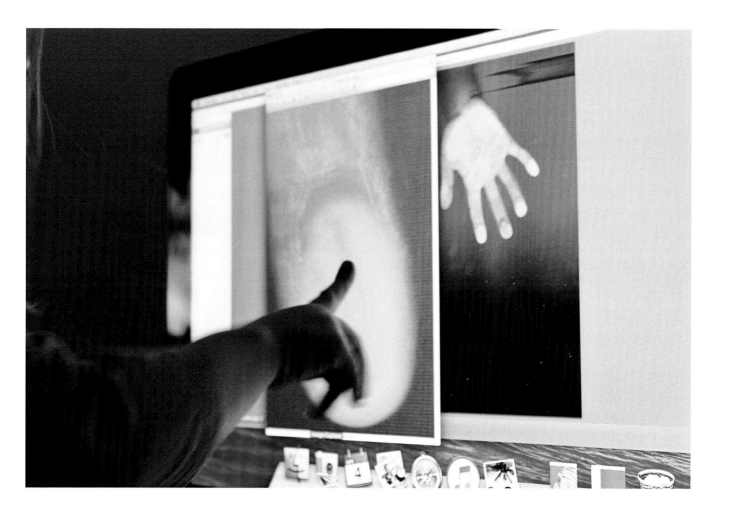

When the children sat down to reflect on their investigation they pointed out subtle differences, such as patterns on their fingerprints and colour of their skin.

Charlotte proposes their earlier theory as a queston, **"do we still think our hands are all the same?"**

"No! Our hands are not all the same!" Ria (3.8 yrs)

Much like finger prints, our teeth are unique to each of us. Our research progressed from exploring a sense of identity through finger prints, to exploring teeth.

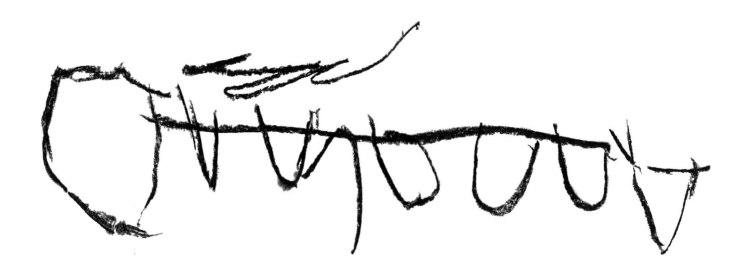

Drawing of tooth xrays by Lara (3.8 yrs)

Receiving a donation of model teeth from a parent provided an interesting way to extend the idea of identity.

"What are these? Where have they come from?" Eden (2.6 yrs)

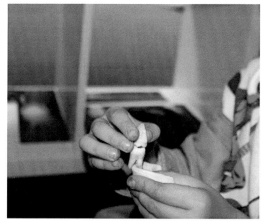

Arthur examines the teeth, closely looking at every angle...

"It seems like that is a teeth and that is a teeth. But I don't know if it's real?" Arthur (2.9 yrs)

Gaining a new perspecive through the microscope allowed the children to build theories and create stories to make meaning...

"There is a hole in this tooth...that's where the jelly people enter... they are called enters"

"Sometimes the jelly people go into the teeth with their little jelly hammers, that's why there is a hole in the teeth, they make sure your teeth aren't hurting"

"There are brain people too, they are different to the jelly teeth people, the brain people are little red people and the jelly teeth people are white" Lucas P (3.9 yrs)

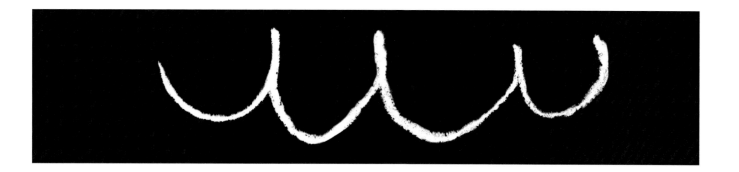

"I can see the inside!"

"And there's my teeth on the screen!" Lucas M (3.11 yrs)

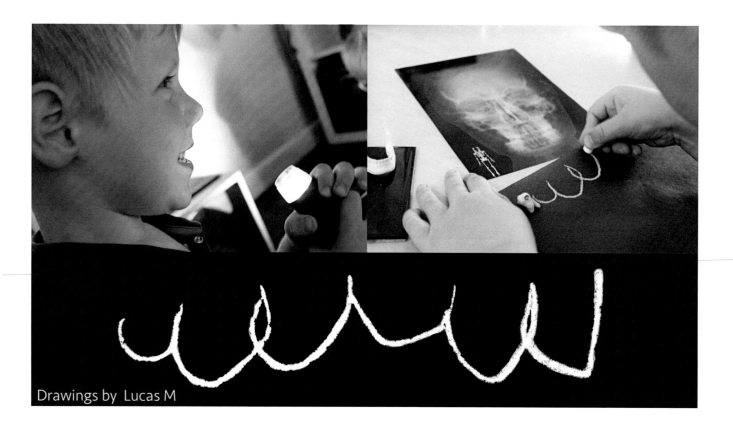

Drawings by Lucas M

"There are lots of little people in your brain and when you hurt yourself, like your leg, they go down

to your leg to check if you're okay. The brain people go all around the body" Lucas P (3.9 yrs)

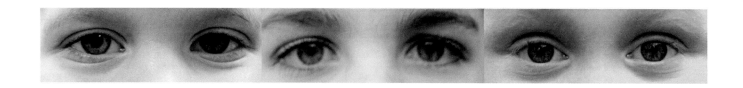

"Are our eyes the same?" Ruby (3.10 yrs)

"They are the same, mine and yours look the same" Ria (3.8 yrs)

"Oh, well what colour are our eyes then?" Ellis (4.5 yrs)

After this question arose, Jodie (educator) suggested to the children they use the digtal cameras and a laptop to take pictures of their own and their friend's eyes and get a closer look.

Ellis was keen to use the camera. Putting the strap around his neck and looking through the lens, Ellis pointed the camera towards his friends faces. Jodie explained that it is polite to ask the children if he could take their photograph and explain why he is taking it.

Ellis asked Julie (another educator) and once she'd agreed, he took her photo. He looked at the photo.

"She's too far away, I need to go closer"

He stepped closer, holding out his hands…

"This close, nearly touching her"

He took the photo again and seemed happy with the result. Each time Ellis took a photo of someone's eyes, he ensured he was 'this close' using his hand to measure.

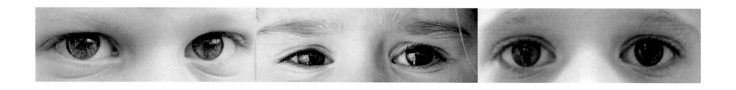

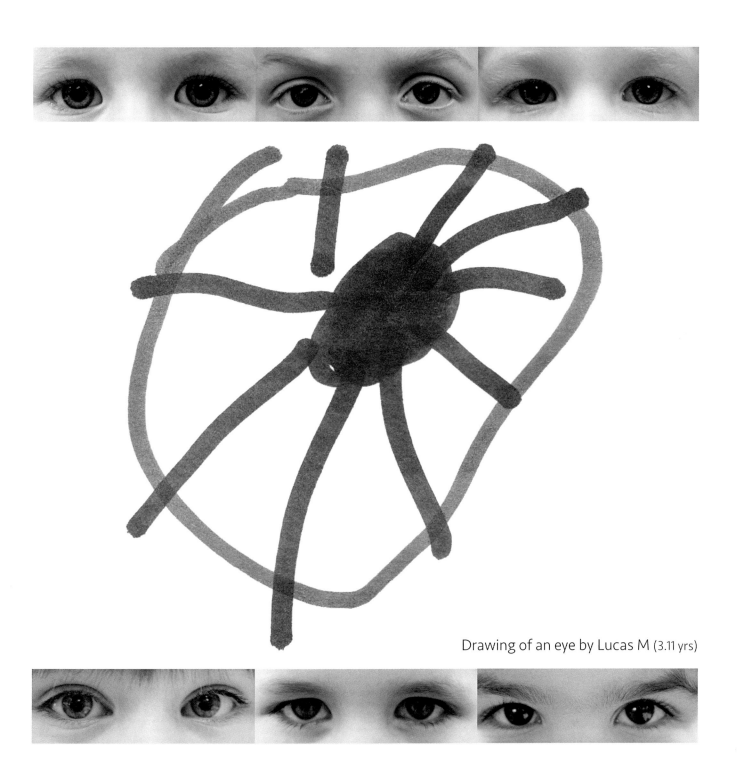

Drawing of an eye by Lucas M (3.11 yrs)

Skeletons and X-rays

During one of our morning meetings the children began to exchange ideas about bones. To provoke the children's thinking we projected a video of a moving skeleton.

Drawing by Isobel (4.2 yrs)

Sculpting the Skeleton

After talking about skeletons, observing and moving in time to the skeleton video projection, and spending time looking at a small skeleton model, an educator suggests that they work together as a group to sculpt a skeleton, bringing together all of their developed understanding.

Archie (3.8 yrs) suggests making the spine first, and after manipulating the wire for a few minutes he turns a chair upside down and begins wrapping the wire around to create a spiralled effect with the wire.

Afer sculpting a spine and a skull the children begin using wire to represent and sculpt other bones in the body for their model.

Ellis (4.5 yrs) decides he wants to sculpt the hand bones and asks for a piece of paper. With some support Ellis draws around his hand and cuts wire to the size of each finger, laying them on the drawing to compare size.

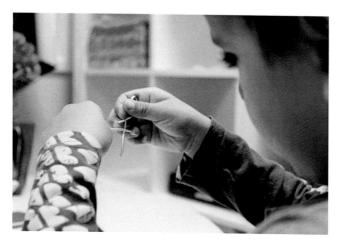

Ellis then connects all of the wire together to form a hand for the wire skeleton sculpture.

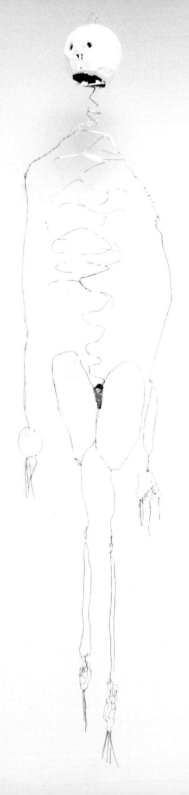

A photograph of the wire skeleton sculpted by the children in the preschool.

Skeleton Sculpture

The children shared ideas and about the parts of the skeleton they would need to create with wire, branching off into research together - looking at books, photographs and videos - to discover which part of the skeleton to sculpt next. The children permanently have access to wire as a resource within the preschool environment, and use this language of expression as a way to share their skills and techniques, supported by the educators and the Atelierista (artist working with children). The collaborative skeleton took a month to complete, with the children revisiting it each day.

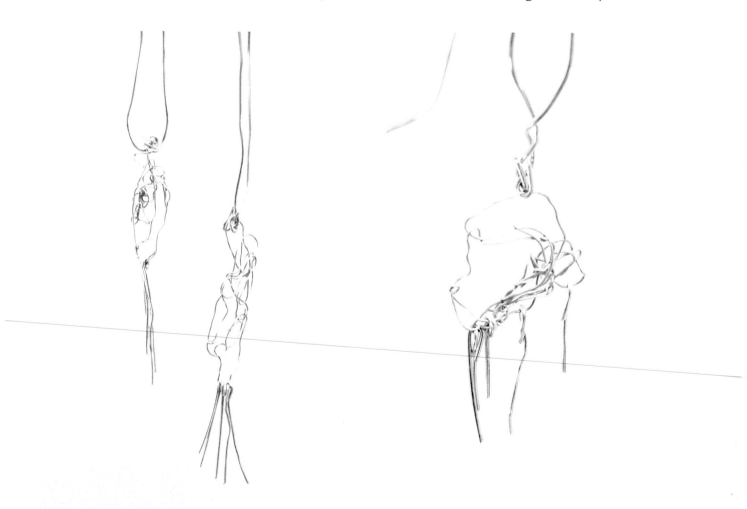

Animal Skulls

Understanding the children's particular interest in skeletons, we decided to loan some animal skulls from a local museum. The animal bones we rented included a warthog skull, pig skull and fox skull.

The children were fascinated by the skulls. They used magnifying glasses to look closely at the bones and observational drawing materials to document what they saw.

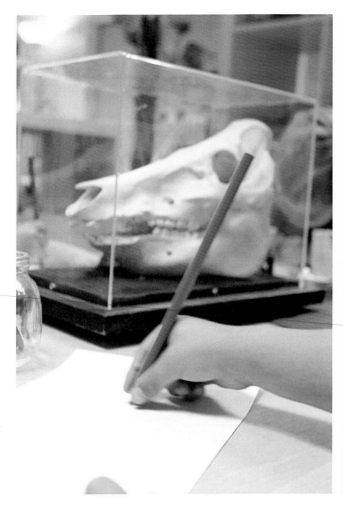

Chalk

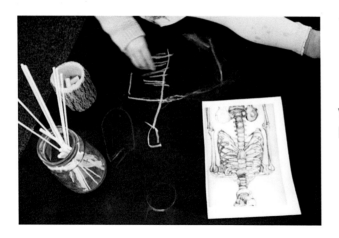

Whilst drawing, Grace (3.6 yrs) shared her story about how a skeleton becomes visible...

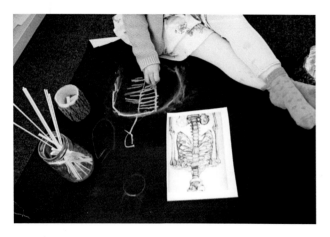

"This is a boat. It's a dead boat. The sun makes it dry and that's what makes it a skeleton boat."

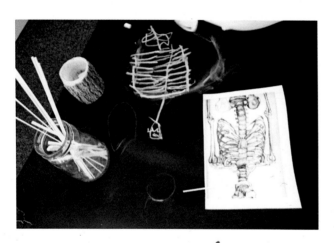

"There is a lady who wanted to buy the boat, but the sun dried it up and it turned to a skeleton."

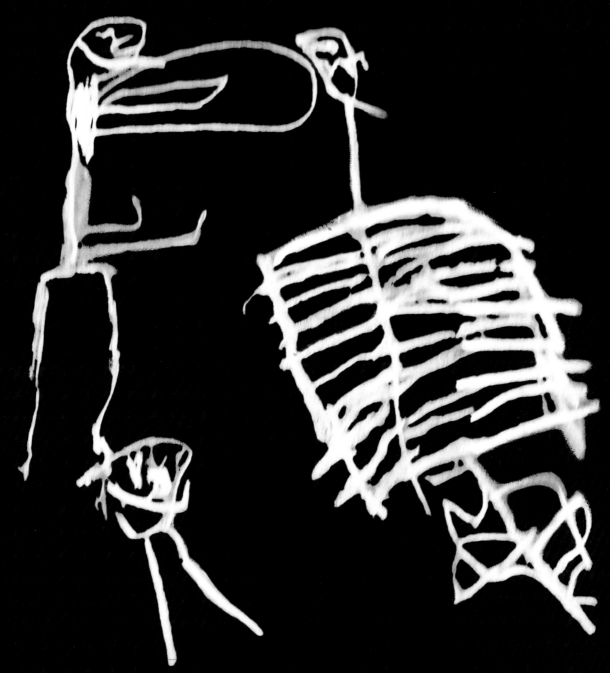

Drawing by Grace

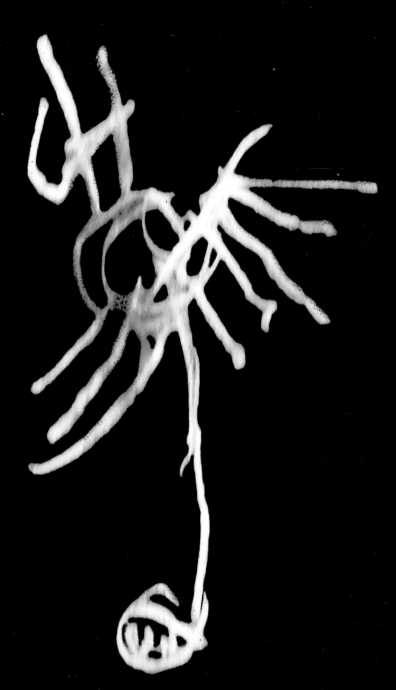

Grace (3.6 yrs) begins to draw a flower...

"I'm drawing a buttercup skeleton"

"Do plants and flowers have skeletons?" Charlotte (educator)

Grace studies the flowers stem...

"I think they do!"

Drawing by Grace

The idea that plants have skeletons was a theory that became interesting for the children to explore...

Using light, a digital microscope and a webcam, alongside laptops and magnifying glasses lent a new perspective for the children.

They began testing the theory that plants have skeletons.

"It feels like its got bones... The teeny tiny lines must be bones!" Beth (4.5 yrs)

Thea uses the digital microscope, shining it onto the head of a sun flower while Ria watches the laptop screen.

"I can see it Thea, keep going. There it is, the skeleton!" Ria (3.8 yrs)

"Its hard, it looks a bit like a bone!" Lara (3.8 yrs)

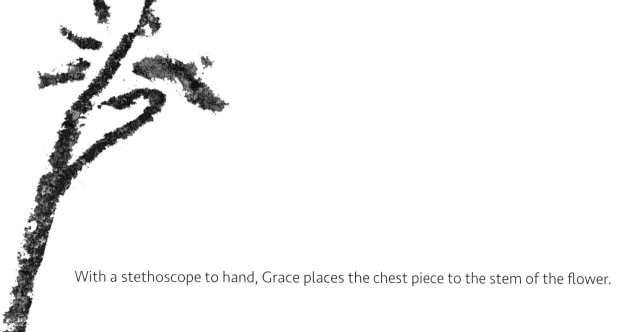

With a stethoscope to hand, Grace places the chest piece to the stem of the flower.

"I can hear the bumpity bump!"

Drawing by Grace (3.6 yrs)

Thoughts, Dreams & Memories

Reflecting on Beth's original quote, **"worlds in our heads, tunnels in our minds"**, we knew the interest wasn't limited to our biological and anatomical make up, but also in our imagination, emotions and feelings. We shared 'imagination art' with the children. Instantly the children reacted, commenting on the feelings of the people in the images.

Looking at the imagination art images...

"That's exciting! Like a firework"
Lara (3.8 yrs)

"She's happy, she's got lots of colour!"
Beau (3.10 yrs)

"I'm drawing my thoughts" Lucas M (3.11 yrs)

Lucas often chooses to draw to express himself, reminding us of the uniqueness of every child and the individual strategies they employ to make sense of the world.

Drawings by Isobel S (4.2 yrs)

After proposing Lucas's idea of drawing thoughts to the other children,

"I'm just thinking about being good" Isobel S

Drawing and sculpting Memories

"A memory is something that wiggles around your body!" Maddie H (3.1 yrs)

"I lost my memories, I think they fell on the floor" Maia (2.11 yrs)

Thinking About Thinking

"We need to keep all these thinks safe!"

After representing thoughts, feelings and memories through drawing, materials were provided to represent our thoughts in another way.

Ellis (4.5 yrs) starts by composing materials to represent his thoughts...

Choosing a flower, **"this helps me think!"** he shares as he pulls the petals and sprinkles them in a frame. **"They're all my *thinks* and they help me think more!"**

A button and mosaic tile are wrapped in string... **"This makes me laugh!"**

Ellis coughs loudly, as he does he grabs a pencil and paper and draws. **"This is to make me cough... even my coughs can go in there!"**

He collects a picture he drew previously of a brain and hands and wants to add them. **"Even these!"**

Ellis looks concerned **"We need to keep all these *thinks* safe, they can fall!"**

"How about in a jar?" Educator

Ellis carefully moves his 'thinks' into a jar, covering it with fabric because **"they might come out the top."**

Thinking Jars

Ellis's desire to 'protect his *thinks*' inspired us to propose his idea of a 'thinking jar' to the other children. The jars became a way for the children to comfortably talk about, recognise and represent, their 'thinks', feelings and worries.

Lara (3.8 yrs) interested in the concept of representing her thoughts, decided to find herself a jar. She began by picking up the orange wool. She wound the wool around her palm, cut it to her desired length then slipped it off her hand and added it to her jar. **"Not happy Lara! Some times I not happy!"** She told me with a stern look and serious voice. **"That's not happy!"** she said whilst pointing to her jar, still wearing a frown.

Next, Lara chose blue wool and held it over her jar. She began to snip tiny bits off and watched them as they fell into her jar. Her facial expression changed to a smile as she told me **"that's happy, lots of little happys!"** Whilst adding more and more Lara tells me, **"Okay, the sad is at the bottom and the happy is at the top!"**

Lara then takes a moment to examine the outside of her jar. She picks up a pen and makes small, precise circles on the outside. **"These are messages to Mummy, I love my Mummy!"**

A week later Lara (3.8 yrs) gets her jar. She carefully cuts pink wool.

"I'm adding bonkers, I'm lots of bonkers!" she says with a giggle.

Her face changes and she chooses some blue string, some **"sad."**

"Just needs to be small, cos I hurt Holly and Mummy told me 'No' that's sad so I put that in there", she says as she carefully puts the string in the jar.

Ellis's (4.5 yrs) and Lara's thinking jars show different thoughts and processes. Ellis has mostly represented physicality and practicality, whereas Lara has represented emotions, relationships and real experiences.

Bethany (4.5 yrs) and Dylan (4.4 yrs) entered the digital atelier to explore a session with the digital microscope. Dylan tells Bethany, **"you know Bethany, you can see your brain when you put it on your head!"**

"Brains are for thinking", says Bethany. She then pauses before saying, **"can I just go and get something?...I'll be right back".**

Bethany returns after a few moments later holding her thinking jar - a collection of thoughts that she has been building up in a jar over the past week or so.

"This is my thinking jar. I cant read yet, and that's okay, I can just draw what I'm thinking and put it in the jar.. I want to draw me as a fire fighter when I'm older, I'm going to be a funny fire fighter", says Bethany (4.5 yrs).

"Can I put a thought in your thinking jar Bethany?", asks Dylan (4.4 yrs).

"Yes, you can. We need small bits of paper though, lets go and get some", replies Bethany.

"I'm going to draw my thought about going to school", says Dylan.

Conclusion

The documentation in this book aims to celebrate the learning processes of children and make visible the construction of knowledge that has been gained in self-propelled and creative ways. Lucas explained his theory about 'jelly enters' that look after our teeth. His theory is an example of the divergent way children are making sense of themselves and the world around them through making stories to share their understanding. A particularly interesting process in the project was the idea of '*keeping thinks safe*' and homing emotions and ideas. The 'thinking jars' became a curative way for the children to represent their thoughts and emotions. The jars became precious little capsules of questions and reflections about their personalities too – being funny, sad, happy, and naughty all featured as did their relationships with people closest to them. The jars were kept on shelves that were easily accessible for children to use materials, scribe notes and add to as they wished. Lara demonstrated the strength of her connection with her thinking jar by sharing her '*thinks*' with an educator many months later, recalling and naming the representation of the feelings and thoughts she had added 10 months before.

The project became a vehicle for children to research themselves, in both an anatomical and metacognitive way. There was more opportunity to make sense of 'self' as they began to 'think about thinking' and further to recognise that they were becoming conscious of their thoughts and feelings and able to develop ways to reflect on them. John Flavell, researcher of metacognition, talks of three main areas that human beings need awareness: an awareness of knowledge – understanding what we know; an awareness of thinking – understanding cognitive tasks and selecting strategies for a task; an awareness of thinking strategies – self assessing and understanding approaches to learning. All too often we can get caught up on 'what to learn' instead of 'how to learn'. Our approach is committed to showing solidarity to children and the unique strategies they employ to build knowledge for themselves. For us, the process of learning, the process of thinking, and the process of *learning* to learn is what we are truly interested in.

We think all children's ideas and theories are rich and full of learning potential. We also believe that children have the right to express their opinions. We dedicate ourselves to providing a comfortable environment to allow children to share their thoughts. Whilst researching identity and the theory that 'our hands are the same' children embarked on a collaborative learning process. Through different languages of expression and digital technology, the children worked together to research finger prints leading them to share their different theories about what makes us different from one another. Supporting the children to confidently express their opinions gives opportunities for respectful relationships and strengthens democratic practice. After sharing their theories about their hands, the children concluded that "*our hands are not the same.*"